AF251887

Song of Life

By Bernadette L. Shih

生命之歌

East West Discovery Press

Published by:
East West Discovery Press
P.O. Box 2393, Gardena, CA 90247
Phone: 310-532-1115, Fax: 310-768-8926
Website: www.eastwestdiscovery.com

Book and cover design: Albert Lin

Library of Congress Cataloging-in-Publication Data

Shih, Bernadette L.
Song of life / by Bernadette L. Shih.-- 1st ed.
p. cm.
ISBN-13: 978-0-9701654-3-5
ISBN-10: 0-9701654-3-9
I. Title.
PS3569.H4868S65 2005

2005014570

ISBN-13: 978-0-9701654-3-5
ISBN-10: 0-9701654-3-9

First edition 2005
Printed in China
Published in the United States of America

Song of Life

By Bernadette L. Shih

Table of Contents

When one of my friends asked me how old I was, I just smiled and said, "Unfortunately, my friend, not old enough to be truly wise, but fortunately not too young to think I know it all."

At this juncture in life, I have just enough wisdom to realize that life is made up of certain elemental passions and necessities, and that I am not just a product of my environment; that beyond the senses, there is a world of the spirit. Furthermore, I can still retain my capacity for solitude and contentment in the midst of adversities and suffering.

As a Chinese American, I am blessed with the benefits of two cultures: the age-old wisdom of China and the dynamics of the young, vibrant America. Moreover, I am aware of the two disparate sides of human thought and of the possibility of bringing together these divergent ideals into a synthesis that would lead me closer to a workable balance in my attitude toward life.

When my novella, "Love: Leap of the Heart and a Sweet Tear", written in poetry and prose, was published, one of my more pragmatic friends, an electrical engineer, said to me, "Wow! So you decide to come down to earth from your cloud nine, eh?! And to fight your windmills, Don Quixote style! Wow! Do you know that Emily Dickinson wrote 1,775 poems and only seven of them were published in her lifetime?"

"There is no money in poetry, you know that?"

"Yes, I know that. But is there poetry in money!"

My grandmother, whose bound feet were no more than four inches long but who was every bit a great lady, had instilled in me the courage to do what I do best, even if it meant tackling the most difficult task at hand.

"Study hard, Little Bing," Grandmama used to say to me after each story hour—she would tell stories to her seventy-five grandchildren (from her six sons and three daughters)—sitting in our big courtyard on a bamboo chair with big, colorful embroidered cushions. "You are deep-thinking and have a way with words, Little Bing. You can make a difference in the world.

"Be compassionate; be loving," she said, lovingly. "Remember, the fewer things you desire, the closer you are to Buddhahood and contentment. But most of all, know yourself, and more importantly, Little One, be true to your inner self. Always!"

Grandmother lived the last years of her life in utter simplicity, preaching charity and helping the village poor.

How wise she was! For years later, when I studied Western philosophy and literature, I found out that Socrates had also said, "Those who want the fewest things are nearest to the Gods."

Yes, Grandmama, I have tried hard, studied hard, tried to be good, loving, and compassionate. I try to know myself. But it's frightening, Grandmama. If I know myself too well, I might have to run away! For I am only human, with all my human frailties and imperfections. And as Issa, the great Japanese poet, said: "Where there are humans, you'll find Buddhas and flies!"

On the other hand, if I can but touch one heart with my poetry, I shall not have struggled in vain.

And this I know, Grandmama:
you are sitting
on my Cloud Nine tonight
looking down at me
smiling

Bernadette L. Shih

SONG OF LIFE

Alone
All I can embrace is my sorrow
emotions and passion
from the highest elation to the deepest
despair
Before me
a screen
misty mountains and clear water
reflecting your eternal smile
Soundless
I listen to the echo of my heart
Suddenly
shooting star of fiery passion
darting forth in ecstasy
shattering the expanse of sea and sky
Explosive sounds
bittersweet
burst with past joy and sorrow
Between the beginning and the end
let the elixir of our yearning
be buried deep in our bosom
yet let not our hearts grow cold as stone
on the edge of our soul

Your wish
my silent promise
Joy and sorrow
the foundation of our paradise
Drying my icy tears
I am ready to sing our song of life

AT THE GATE OF PARADISE

Seasons come and go
Soon autumn will be upon us

Memories
veiled by mist and lingering clouds
causing bitter tears to run down
my shivering cheeks

In my garden of summer splendor
early autumn wind whistles sadly
sinking deep into the abyss of my being

Like dust
I am blown about in all directions
swinging between dreams and illusions

Sorrows come
Memories weigh me down

A lost bird
I long for my own forest of eternal joy

Choked by reverie

I ache for lost moments forever gone

Am I condemned
to a life of wandering alone in darkness
infinity touches the edge of my yearning heart

Will glimmer of light fall upon my wretched paths
and I would wait not forever
at the gate of paradise

BELOVED MOTHER

In a silent churchyard
Heaven weeps
You leave on a foggy afternoon
with lost memories on your brow
and looking back not at the setting sun
Beloved Mother
You leave for good and never will return
though you have won the crown of everlasting life

On your last day
Pain reigns supreme
giving love, solitude
and the face of death
We feel your breath on our eyes
and the mouth against our hearts
Whispering
Sleep and dream without me, my children
for the sun is gone from my journey on earth

Beloved Mother
Your leaving left me shaking with tears
on an island of orphans
where I walk daily on the edge of sorrow

and loneliness
Accepting a crown of thorns
bending my head toward my heart
beating with the harsh clang of reality
God's daughter hurls against the cliffs in rage
soundless and remote is my blissful world

CHEERS

Joys of the season

Up into the towering heavens
        our spirits soar

Undaunted
        no worldly cares claim us
Sharing the same dream
        then as now
The bliss of passion
        permeates our hopes
Our destiny
        like blue clouds over the hills
                boundless water and sky

Ne'er for a moment
        we cease to care, to struggle
Strength, born of love's unselfish ways
        sustains and nurtures our souls
Our mind, in tune with nature's creation
        marvels in its beauty and splendor
Our hearts, in harmony
        amidst toils and cares

Our love, unwavering
this we will forever share

CITY OF ANGELS WITH NO WINGS

Sleepless
Alone with my thoughts
as another spring night descends
Sad cry of passing boats drifts across ocean waves
in concert with longings of my sorrowful dirge

Thoughts of you my dearest Father
like an eagle
sweeps me up on its mighty wings
Upon heavenly clouds I sit
looking down on a city that has lost its soul

City of Angels
Too brief the moment
your respite from violence and crime
Ear-splitting sounds
muffling screams like daggers
pierce the darkness of this darkest night

Fear and lawlessness shroud
this city once so beautiful and bright
Reckless men wander among rosy shadows
like homeless demons

pillaging, killing and raping
in a world gone mad

Blind to the Eternal Way
we plunder on

Tears fall when I wake
and hear your parting word
in all its boundless wisdom

Love and be loved, my children
Honor your father and mother
Abide by the Golden Rule
And be one with nature
Disgrace not the good name of your ancestors
And do unto others what you would have others do unto you

CITY OF ANGELS WITH NO WINGS

Surely your spirit of light will leap across the sea
    rearing its colossal weight into the darkening sky
Evil darkness of night
    will soon fade from every hill and dale

The City of Angels will once again be serene
    and prosper along the banks of the shimmering
        Pacific

For you, my Father
    have taught me to see beauty
        human eyes have never seen
            and given strength to force open
                the gate of Paradise

A chaotic world made harmonious
Wondrous still are man and nature as one

I have touched all things with enchanted hands
And feel eternally in my soul
    Beauty and love
For all
I sing

The song of life triumphant
SATORI
ALLELUIA, ALLELUIA

EDGE OF ETERNITY

Love, tender
        the lucidity of calm waters
Emotion, fragile
        the wings of a cicada

"Bye, My Sweet,"
        you whisper

Our bodies, naked
        tremble on the edge of a dream
                I do not see
Our spirit, free
        ascend onto the edge of heaven
                I do not know

"Bye, My Sweet,"
        I linger

Tears of parting
        stream down our faces
                glistening in the moonlight

Body and spirit as one

we fly to the eternal Void
where birth is not a beginning
nor death an end

EDEN OF MY DREAM

A spring breeze
        sweeps across the garden of my heart
The multicolor roses you planted
        are vibrantly fragrant with fulfillment

Today I want to take you
        to the Eden of my dream

Where Mozart composes his symphonies
        on a PC
Where Bill Gates listens to Beethoven's Sixth
        by a bubbling brook on an ancient Victrola

Where Hitler, Stalin and Bin Laden
        preach not their ideology of hatred and
                discrimination
                        but sing songs of love and compassion

Where Mao takes not those fateful great leaps forward
        nor condones the butcheries of the Great Cultural
                Revolution

Where no banners of such ill intent are ever raised over

Vietnam, Bosnia, Rwanda, Somalia, Kosovo
Jerusalem and Tienanmen Square

Instead
We are all children again
living in a childlike world
Where we sing and dance
with Jesus, Buddha, Lao Tzu
Lincoln, Gandhi and Martin Luther King
to tunes of Love, Peace, and Harmony

END OF THE BEGINNING

From within a stormy heart
        comes a gentle stirring
Years we share each other's problems
Shed each other's tears
Vent each other's anger
Rise to heaven and down to hell
        in each other's arms

Spring buds, summer blossoms
Autumn leaves, winter snow
Music, books
Sushi, Moo-shu pork
        of which pleasures we partake
Respect, affection, love from all germinate
Passion
        now ripples in a vast sea of calm and serenity

End of the beginning
For us
        a new dawn

EU TE AMO

As we walk up and down life's winding path
your love wholly fills me still
my galloping steed

Let go not our tightening grasp
as we lean on each other to live in fervent intensity

I feel joy stirring deep within like a subterranean spring
Today for me is just as beautiful as the many yesterdays we
shared

The seed of passion roots amidst toils and troubles
It's as though I were in front of a wonderful landscape
and see not only mountains and rivers
but white clouds forever drifting in a clear
blue sky

Eu te amo, I love you

FRIENDS

How steep
The road to friendship
is climbing stairs to heaven
World affairs trouble our hearts
and
Shadows of emotion often darken our vision
but
Defying conventions
We are at once sun and moon
casting brilliance upon each other's
substance and style
like stars blinking in an autumn sky

We dare plant flowers in barren grounds
so that
their splendor will last a thousand years
Our path is filled with
sadness and laughter
sorrows and joy
anger and contentment

Darkness and light alternating
It has taken us years to accept

each other with humility and detachment
Giving inspirations
neither with claims nor burden

Friends
One soul in two bodies
stand silent at the water's edge
Waves roll in swiftly
and spread shining on the sand
beneath our feet
Clusters of clouds
pile one upon another
grand but strange
a mass so heavy with light borne in
the air

Light and shade
interchangeable
cloaked in form

FRIENDS

Dark passions
sanctified and shaped by reasons
radiant but structured as in music we share

Spirit of the sea
flows through us
far wider and changeless than the changing
earth
Their thunder
like the intense quiet of
the summer sun

Turbulence! Tranquility!
A lyrical transformation
of waves into ripples upon a violent land

Satori!
Two friends
loving and caring
free to embrace the universe
and call it our own

FROM BOSNIA: A MOTHER'S PRAYER

I cradle my dying child in my arms
And watch a fiery ball fall from Heaven
        blazing, merciless
                engulfing all in its path

Beneath my feet
Demons oozing oil of death
        from their monstrous caldrons
Like flowing lava
Breath of death
        covers the bowels of the earth

Hellish are the great fire and the volcanic lava
        that turn sweetness and innocence to ashes

My child gazes at me with fearful eyes
        which
Yesterday, smiling, reflected trees and flowers
        growing in parks and meadows
                adorning this lovely earth

Today, in the hands of tyrants
Down into the abyss

slides their ring of destruction
Hatred and greed
the ripe bitterness of hemlock
dripped in beads from every tree
into the open wounds of all innocents
Death finds its ready victims

Pain and suffering baptize my child
Flowers and trees lose their beautiful petals
as though made of dust
crumble away

All around
Desolation, darkness
A cemetery
scattered limbs, mangled flesh
Stench of hell's fury
fills my nostrils

FROM BOSNIA: A MOTHER'S PRAYER

Love, sunshine
        forever gone
The world
        Like the devil's laughter
                is empty

My sweet child looks at me with pleading eyes
"Mama, hold me close to your breast
        so tight I would need nothing."
His tiny body convulses
And with a faint smile on his lips
He asks in a fading whisper
"When will I again play in the park?"

O Great Almighty One
"When will I again play in the park?"
Do you not hear my cry for mercy
Silence the voices of history's dark past
Napoleon and Imperial Japan
Hitler and Stalin

Replay not
The Rape of Nanking and the Siege of Leningrad

The Death Camps of Auschwitz and the Gulags of Siberia

Let peaceful voices of
Lao Tzu, Gandhi and Martin Luther King
ring out their mellifluous songs

Shed not one more drop of blood
The same color red
from faces dark or fair

All is just under Heaven
Brothers and Sisters
One voice, One song
Love, Peace and Harmony

I AM A SLAVE NO MORE

Covered by a veil
The past
        a remote reincarnation
                erased forever from memory

What will I be tomorrow?
I do not know
I do not care

This splendid moment
        permeated with joy
        contentment fills my whole being

I am standing in this magic kingdom of everlasting love
        I have no need for fame or fortune
        All I desire is to laugh at myself and my follies
        I know nothing
        I possess nothing
        I desire nothing

I am once again a child
        merrily singing in praise of nothingness
                the fullness of life

A caged bird burst out from within
happily flying toward the land of the free

MEMORY OF GRANDMOTHER

In the vast country of life
        I wander, lost
Seeking for truths my Grandmother had told

I look in the sunrise for light
Search for hope in the setting sun
Alone on a sunny shore
In the shadow of a lonely mountainside
I hear only echoes of a solitary bird in flight
        as a single cloud drifts by
Silent breath of night
        sweeps across this foreign land
                my soul so loves as though I had no native
                        home

Memories of Grandmother
        upon which my thoughts repose
Like countless twilights
        radiant, resplendent
I carry with me from my ancient past

You are woman
Yes, Grandmama, I am woman

Keeper at the gate of paradise
Whisperer of desire in my lover's ear

I am park bench where children can sit
basking in the sun
and drink the warmth from my breast
throbbing with life's eternal blood

I am close to this lovely earth
embracing her rugged terrain
bend murmuring to the ground

Mankind in turmoil
You will feel my sweet breath on your bitter lips
And my tender touch soothing your warring hearts

So sleep and dream my sweet child
this chaotic world
Soon you will wake in peace to kiss a new dawn

JOURNEY HOME

I walk the path of my childhood
endless streams and gentle rolling hills
as chrysanthemums begin to yellow

Footsteps, carefree
mingle with the noises of a thousand ravines

Upon this land I so loved
Strange changes are replacing old customs old beliefs
New thoughts of today
that will not be thoughts of tomorrow

Material wants we make divine
And never in my beloved China
are the teachings of the Ancient Sages
so quickly forgotten
them we have beseeched in our pain
and blessed in our joy

Materialism rages through even the countryside
Rich and poor
Merchants and peasants

suffer from this fever that will not abate

We listen only with our ears
not our mind
Detouring from the pathway
our great ancients had troddened and made
luminous
Forgotten too, is their silent say
in every impulse of our life

My Grandmother's grave is gone now
dug up to make way for a big factory
that makes robots of the young and the old
The blow of modernization has axed our ancient souls
and the Confucian man is no more

I long not for the cling-clang sound of motorcars
but my Grandmother's gentle voice
calling me home from play
in the field of growing green and wild flowers

JOURNEY HOME

I yearn not to hear the sound of televisions
and Nintendo machines
But the mellifluous voices of children
chanting poetry
and the classics from their hearts

Sorrow
arrows of winged bows
pierces my innermost being

Alas!
Dare I dream a dream of spring
when cherry blossoms bloom
linger but a moment's space
and die
In dying
They leave behind the knowledge
that soon again
we will see them in full bloom
Like the China of yore
in all their spiritual magnificence and splendor

JULY FOURTH DAWNS EARLY LIGHT

I wake up
        confused
I do not know
        I do not know
                I know who I am

I can die
        from too-low cholesterol
                or too much exercise

Lost innocence
Unrealistic expectations
Idealized Hollywood gods

Sickly
A society that pays
        athletes, entertainers millions
        and teachers a mere pittance

If I thought you could hear me
        I wouldn't talk
Only a sense of shame
        shall enable us to a sense of limits

Only you, Lord of Truth
luminous
to which all things are drawn

Only you, Almighty Love
when I look into the eyes of a newborn child
that makes the frame of death
give meaning to life

So live
Live life
while I've got it

Talk of the soul
In poetry
truth and beauty roam

JULY FOURTH DAWNS EARLY LIGHT

Touching my very being
Poetry and music
        shall be in all things
                if I have ears
                        and eyes to see

So sing
Sing a song of love and goodness
Henceforth
        I shall live among the brave and the free
Hosanna
Hosanna in the highest

LADY LIBERTY: GODDESS OF MERCY

I am young no more
Vainly I search for the center of my soul
where hope and compassion dwelt
where I could remember without pain
where joyful voices spoke to me of love and peace
where Lady Liberty
Goddess of Mercy sat upon her Lotus
Throne
smiling and scattering cherry
blossoms in my path

She spoke softly
Weep not all ye faithful
for unto your world of gloom
will come a bright star to guide you
into the center of your soul

I am young no more
My children are dying each day
in violent fields of hunger and hate
I cry my prayer to you, Lady Liberty
only to have it bounce back
like echoes from a stone wall

Your Lotus Throne has turned to plaster and gilded wood
Your smile, cynical laughter
        laughing at mothers in despair
Yorktown, Somalia, Bosnia, Rwanda, Haiti, and Kosovo

I lie within a court of silent dreams
        lonely, staring into darkness
The door of hope is enclosed in a tomb of sorrow
My whole being aches for the touch of your merciful hand
        and longs for your whisper of divine promise
                "Unto your world of gloom will come
                        a bright star to guide you into the
                                center of your soul!"

NIGHT GARDEN

I see my reflection in the garden pond
weary, without softness nor wisdom
born of pain and suffering
hollowed eyes, vanished hopes, illusive dreams

I feel like a tree growing in Los Angeles
fighting pollution and dirt
In my sorrow
the gentle night breeze not only whispers in my ears
the distant cry of children dying in their
war-torn countries
but the joyful scream of a newborn child
emerging in blood from the mother's
womb
And I know deep within my breast
beyond sorrow and hopelessness
that birth is not a beginning, nor death an
end

In my garden of solitude
grass and blossoms vie in elegance
flowers entwined in tender boughs

Engulfed in their beatitude
I flow in quiet euphony
Escaped from worldly cares
I feel no compunction for a while
to dwell in the Zen world of my birth

One with nature
carefree, I wander through the heavenly void
gaze at the drifting mist
and listen to the even beat of my heart

In my mind
I see flying geese and leaping fishes
Blossoms are everywhere
rejoicing from the sheer felicity of their beauty

In nature's arms
I watch the moon's soft touch linger
shading each tree branch
as she sails through the shimmering
cloud

NIGHT GARDEN

All that I lack
All that I desire to be
Oneness with nature
It alone can bring peace and contentment

I feel again the depth of passion and joy
I open my eyes to see in life and death
All things beautiful

ORA PRO NOBIS

Passion
Wild, fiery
roams through scorching hearts

Lifting body and soul
to previously unreachable heights
Until
We lie exhausted
in each other's arms
While Eros's golden blood
courses through our lips and our groins

Defying all conventions and norms
the future will cast upon us its fateful shadow
But
For one breathless moment
I see in the horizon
nothing but radiant sun

PACIFIC INTERMEZZO

With one look
You touch and reign
over the fountain of my heart
Plant flowering gardens in my soul
And bestow endless days of sunshine in my life

Now that you are gone
I lie here thinking
Savoring of happiness past
Tender kisses, sweet caress
A fusing of body and mind
East and West in perfect harmony

But when I close my eyes
And hope for things that can never be
A world without borders
Demarcations without walls
Beginning without end
Love without sorrow

An unbearable sadness
Clouds my blue horizon
Vast, dark, foreboding

Our dreams flow out like water
Passion evaporates like dew
Tears fall like rain

O My Fair Adonis
Will you ever return
To quench the yearnings
Of my desolate heart

A PLACE IN THE COUNTRY

A place in the country
I find solace

Not one trace of civilization
dares invade these sacred woods

I look upwards between ancient trees
so mighty and majestic

Body, mind and soul
purged from all complexities
returning to the beginning

Uncluttered and feeling neither joy nor sorrow
I embrace all with detachment

PURE LAND OF JOY

Predawn on a deserted beach
I stretch my legs
Lean back on my hand
And look out to sea

Masses of clouds
appear in the distance
Immense in their quiet majesty
They swallow up noises all around
Save the sound
of your bare feet jogging on the sand

You, too, have come out
at this hour
to avoid anger in the rays of the August sun

You smile at me
And I see your laughing eyes
deep, dark
All encompassing in their loftiness
the impossible dreams of life

We talk of things

Past, present and future
as though floating on the Pure Land of
Buddhahood
Timeless
There is not one ripple to stir
the surface of the Pacific

When I look into your soul
like a single Lotus Flower
spreading out to infinite horizons

All around
Little sea creatures are jumping
intoxicated with delight
A glimmer of light flashes by the Pier
And I think it unfair that a short while ago
I should be so unhappy

PURE LAND OF JOY

Hand in hand
We stand knee-deep in the water
Our eyes sparkle
as we sway to the rhythm of our hearts
feel the sand at the soles of our feet

Water leaps up
breaking into little beads
that glisten upon your naked skin

Your tender smile
brings to my long night
the brightness of dawn
When the bond of fate
will seal us within the gate of Paradise

In warm embrace
happily drifting
We will bring each other great joy

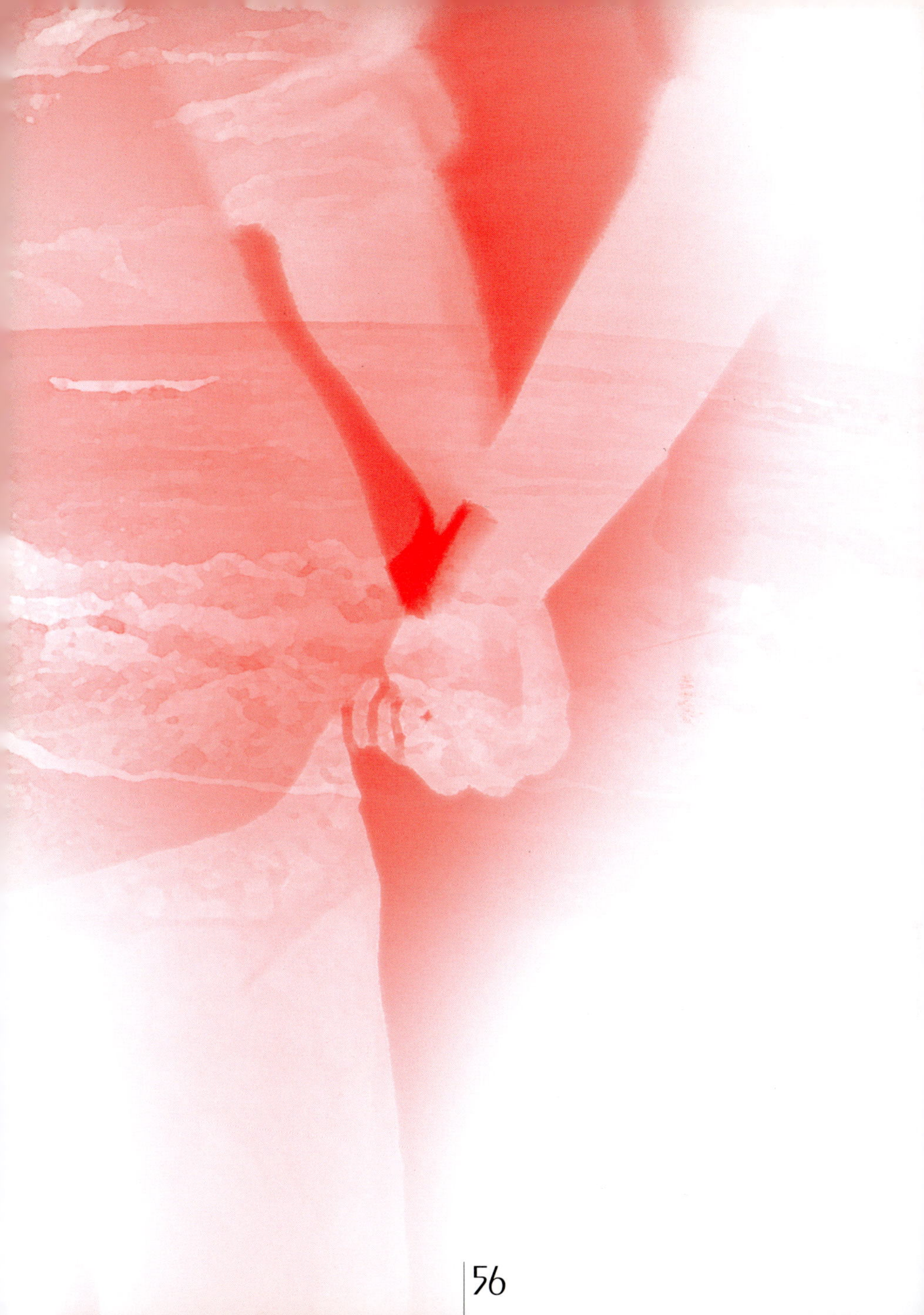

SCARLET ROSES

In my burning hand
	I hold your scarlet rose with thorns

Trembling
	I am alone on a sunny shore
		feeling your burning kiss on my shivering lips

I am lost in the garden of my soul
	watching the lingering moon's soft touch
		in concert with the lonely beating of my
			heart

A lone star
	falling on this cold and wonderful night
	slowly sips the warmth from my hand

Love
	smiles in its sleep
	dreaming of eternity
	casting its red rose into a white womb

This night
	a fleeting moment of ecstasy

your heavy head against my tender breast

SEPTEMBER ELEVEN: THIS, TOO, SHALL PASS

It all seems so unreal, almost surreal, what's happening to us. How can some of our fellow human beings harbor so much malice and hatred in their hearts!

With much sadness, but not without hope, I pray.

Forgive us all, Almighty Father!

My wounded child strapped to my back
I crawl through
Dusty alleys
leading to the Gate of Sorrow
glow in the last rays of the setting sun
At the edge of this sorrowful land
the door of death is always open
Trembling bodies
Silent tears fall
from vacant eyes
down to hollow cheeks
disappearing on defenseless faces
Torn by the forces of my sorrow
I cannot move
nor shed my tears
My lips tremble

like leaves in the autumn wind
Battle cry of Talibans and bin Laden disciples
reverberates
mocking the silent echo of
mass graves, swollen corpses, crushed skulls
Out of Lucifer's shadow
A warrior steps forward
pushing my child to the ground
A blinking machete flashes by
splitting my child's head into two
Gushes of blood
Cool spring of life
innocent, angelic

SEPTEMBER ELEVEN: THIS, TOO, SHALL PASS

Like mist
blinds my vision of total destruction
incinerating my soul with the heat of a thousand
suns
and escapes in a blaze of golden glory

Words I am too weak to utter
sink deep in my heart

Almighty Father
Have mercy on us all

SEPTEMBER SONG

In life's journey
We cross mountains
Leap along rocky shores
And grope in shadows
        when heaven is veiled by clouds

As we stand in darkness
        unison in body and soul
Love, a spring breeze
        sweeps across our hearts
Strong in our traditions
        old and new
Patiently waiting, bending
Yet daring to climb upwards against the wind
Until the sky above opens
        shedding light to guide us into a world
                within a million worlds
Where our spirits will once again
Soar
Atop a mountain in the sun

SHIP OF FOLLIES

Love
Sanctified
A thing of more than beauty
Its passion
        a far-away sun
                has turned golden trees to flame

In solitude
The autumn winds
        wail sadly
                sending adrift
                        a shining leaf
                                looking for a home

My heart
A stray butterfly
        blown hither and thither
                by the lusty winds of desire

Longing, searching
I sail my ship of follies
        across the stormy sea of love

SILENT KISS

Distant clouds
misty
wisping from the bowels of mountains
Ascending
blending with the heavens
in blue-green harmony

Below
water cascading through forest of majestic pines
striking rocks and pebbles

Singing
joyous songs of an autumn day

SOLITUDE

Emptiness
heavy
saying nothing

Stars
a silvery crown
twinkling coldly

Noises of night
soft whispers
as though they know my sorrow

Sadly
the cry of croaking frogs
and chirping crickets

They, too, have come
to join me
in my song of life

Silently
I turn away
smiling from love

SUDDEN THUNDER

Emotions
        mountain torrents dashing at my heart
                breaking walls, boundaries with bitter joy

Gale winds
        wreaking havoc in a sea of tranquility

My Yellow River
        will one day again be calm?

For now
I am a butterfly
        journeying to the corners of the universe
                where only your smile awaits me
                where mountain streams and valley brooks
                        flow into rivers and seas
                where I tear not on the edge of your sleeves
                        but spit my sorrow to the wind

THANKSGIVING

All around me
darkness
bleak, unfathomable

Autumn's falling leaves
swept away
ushering in the cold wind
of winter snow

A solitary wanderer
drifting along paths of icy flakes

In this deserted edge of winter wonderland
I abandon
all my sorrow
unfulfilled dreams
in pursuit of spiritual serenity
life's true happiness
and the beginning of my
journey
to eternal joy

TILL NEXT TIME

Pain
born in my heart
stays with me at the door
when we say good-bye
Sobs
caught in my throat
pierce my chest
and ache in my belly

Tonight
I do not sing
but weep

For your leaving
I have written songs
for my tears

VIS VITAE

Yes
I want to shout from the rooftops that
I have forgotten
Even though it had taken me so very long to forget

As memories fade farther into the past
Time, by its miracle, brings into focus all that had happened
And erased all tracks left in my heart

Now
The rails lie silent
No longer do I think of the past with melancholy
Only the present with contentment and tranquility

We do not swear or pledge our undying love
        nor our eternal passion
We only have to look into each other's eyes
        to find peace and serenity
A deep caring that will endure
        as long as we have the courage
                to live and to struggle

I do not feel

your shiver in the wind
your sting in the rain
your heat in the sun

All I feel is you
equilibrium for my faltering ways
dikes for the mighty waves of existence
compass in the open sea

You have planted a seed in me
I will nurture
'til it blossoms and transcends all

Above
The unreachable sky
I see a river of stars
And in my heart
flow a thousand springs

VIS BREVIS

Early morning
I went for a walk
Overcast
red-tiled roofs against misty mountains
The Pacific, a steely grey
casting shadow over the country of my heart
Silently grieving, weeping
'til
Thoughts of you warmed my trembling soul

You rose from beneath the ocean waves
coming close, slowly at first
Then with sudden lightning
sprang toward me
We greeted each other with reserve

Now you stood in front of me
All your manhood glory
tall, strong, confident
God's most perfect creature

A breath of fresh air
blowing away my past

I abandoned all
Our hands joined, lips touched, spirits merged
Two minds fused in desire
Flames incinerated our differences
Tenderness quenched our burning souls
        'til
We plunged into a calming sea
        drowning all obstacles and doubts

We kissed, we fondled
We laughed, we cried
Long silence punctured by gentle murmur
We ascended to heaven
And descended to hell
        in split seconds of eternity
Floating on rainbow-colored clouds

VIS BREVIS

To reality
I waved to mothers driving children
        on their paper routes in shiny Mercedes
Time to finish my jog

Ahead
Confusing turns
        perhaps leading to a nowhere land
But
        for the moment
I am feeling
        alive
Yearning for your embrace

WAITING

Early rain
patters against the windowsill

Unlike the dreary rain of winter
it sweeps across the mountaintop
dancing, laughing
caressing my happy face

Waiting
I hear not your footsteps across the room
over the fierce beating of a longing heart

YOU

New pulse of life
beating through quiet veins

A spring morn
giving new buds
to help forget the barren earth of winter

I wake with hope
listening to the song of a meadowlark

My whole being
bathed in joy
Thinking of your lips
I kissed in my dream

YOUNG LOVE

I whisper your name
only within my heart
For
I am swept away into the land
of our golden dreams

You will come to me from yonder hills
And sing songs of water
falling from far-away mountain streams

Lonely cry of two flutes in harmony
tuned to pitch from distances far apart

I feel again
of years gone by
Shimmering water murmuring
beneath lotus flowers
that would speak to me of your love

Kings in their palace grow old
Your love
will forever dwell young
in the contentment of my heart

POET'S JOY

O such spiritual joy
All day
I have been writing
    overcoming
        loneliness
        regrets
            of unfulfilled dreams
            incomplete tasks
        Burdens
            of unshakable responsibilities

Am I toiling yet on another unmarketable script
    I don't care

I have looked for a flower
    and found a blossom
I have longed for a well
    and found a sea
I have searched for a girl
    and found a woman

Today
I have found myself

a step toward freedom and truth
Merrily I shrug off disappointment with a chuckle
Life goes on
Another leaf
Another chapter

My soul stretches its arms
higher than all the heavens
I am close to everything
and God Himself